I quit the art class.

It was a little too sketchy.

Doctor: "I think your DNA is backwards."

Me: "AND?"

A quick shout-out to all the sidewalks out there:

Thanks for keeping me off the streets.

What's the worst Dad joke ever?

This one!

How are opera singers and sailors alike?

They both have to handle the high C's!

Why was Santa's tiny helper feeling depressed?

Because he had low elf-esteem.

What do dentists call their x-rays?

Tooth pics!

Did you hear about the bankrupt poet?

He ode everyone.

What did Adam say on the 24th of December?

It's Christmas Eve.

A sandwich walked into a bar. The barman said, 'Sorry, we don't serve food in here.'

I just burned 2000 calories. Serves me right for having a nap while the brownies were cooking in the oven.

How do the Chinese make a beer recipe?

With a brewprint.

I surprised my wife with a mink coat. She'd never seen me in one before.

I went to the doctor's to ask if he had anything for the wind.

So he gave me a kite.

I'll tell you about an actor who's rubbish.

Dustbin Hoffman.

I saw this film about prehistoric pigs - Jurassic Pork'.

'Doctor, I think I'm a cat.' 'How long's this been going on?'

'Since I was a kitten.'

He never smiles. Not because he's got bad teeth. It's just that his gums don't fit.

My dog has an attitude. He is a cocky spaniel.

Going to bed with music gave me a sound sleep.

What did the flame tell his parents when he fell in love? I've found the perfect match!

What is a zucchini's favorite game?

Squash.

How do hurricanes see?

With one eye

Why do kangaroos love koalas?

Because they have many fine koalaties!

How do you tune a fish?

With its scales!

What does the frog in Paris eat?

French Flies!

Who's a cow's favorite person?

Youuuuuu!

I just interviewed for a waiter job at my favorite restaurant. I hope they saw that I could bring a lot to the table.

There was an inspirational song playing in the car that kept telling me to go the extra mile. Now I'm out of gas, and I don't know where I am.

Did you hear that train that just went by?

It left tracks.

Kid: "Ow! That hurt!" Dad: "What's wrong?" Kid: "I stubbed my toe!" Dad: "Oh no! Do you want me to call the toe truck?"

What do you call massive marine mammals traveling in huge cars?

Steering whales.

I built a car out of my old sports clothes. You could say it runs Lycra dream.

I just got fired from the flower shop. Apparently, I took too many leaves.

How to get straight A's?

By using a ruler!

I'm practicing for a bug-eating contest, and I've got butterflies in my stomach.

I said to this guy, 'Is there a B and Q in Henley?' He said, 'No, there's an H, E, N, L, and Y.'

I tried to change my password to '14 days,' but my computer said it was two week.

The unluckiest person in my family is my uncle. Two weeks after he went blind, his guide dog went deaf.

I sold my guitar today to a bloke with no arms. I asked how it was going to work, and he said, 'I play by ear.'

What anti-perspirant do pessimists use?

Not Sure

Why are pirates so mean?

They just arrrrrr!

I've just finished a ten-week course with my speech therapist, and I can't say thank you enough.

I rang up the amputee helpline, but I got cut off.

I have a friend in North Korea. I said, 'How's things?' He said, 'Can't complain.'

A new EU directive stating that all meat pies should be wrapped in tin has been foiled.

When you make quick-drying cement, there are no hard and fast rules.

I'm making a TV series about plane hijacking.

We just shot the pilot.

Children shouldn't watch big band performances on TV-too much sax and violins.

RIP, Patrick Moore.

No more Mr. Night Sky.

This bloke went to his doctor with a piece of lettuce sticking out of his arse. 'Ah yes,' said his doctor, 'that's just the tip of the Iceberg.'

I just looked outside to check the patriarchy, and apparently, it's reigning men.

I had to get glasses for my phone because I lost all the contacts.

The night club nearby recently contracted a carpenter. He's really tearing up the dance floor.

My company is introducing glass coffins.

MOM: "Horace, I'm running late. Can you fix dinner for the kids?"

DAD: I didn't know dinner was broken! I'm on it!

Plateaus are the highest form of flattery.

What's the worst kind of cat to have?

A catastrophe!

The swordfish is the best-dressed fish.

It always looks sharp!

Have you ever heard of how crazy a squirrel's diet is?

Most will say it's nuts.

I hate insect puns.
They bug the heck out of me.

Why do dogs run in circles?

Because it's hard to run in squares!

Why is six afraid of seven? It's not; numbers aren't sentient and can't feel fear.

My car fell in a ditch today. Didn't want any more cars falling, so I put a car pit over it.

Accordion to a recent survey, inserting musical instruments randomly into sentences often goes unnoticed."

I am the Norse god of mischief, but I don't like to talk about it. I guess you could say I'm Loki.

A couple of yogurt cups walk into a country club, and the bartender says, "We don't serve your kind here." "Why not?" one yogurt cup asks. "We're cultured."

What did the older light bulb say to the younger light bulb? "You're too young to go out tonight."

Why are mummies scared of vacation?

They're afraid to unwind.

I've been watching a channel on TV that is strictly about origami. Of course, it is paper view.

Why do tigers have stripes?

So they don't get spotted!

Why do pirates not know the alphabet?

They always get stuck at "C."

The reason why shipbuilders never galvanize ships is because that would make them zinc.

69% of people find something obscene in every sentence.

I'm in a band called Stuck in the Departure Lounge. Check us out.

Plan to be spontaneous... tomorrow.

A Muslim and a small rodent with an eyepatch are being hunted by police after a robbery.

The only way prisoners can call each other is on cell phones.

There's only one use
for hippies. To hang
your leggies on.

I have a step ladder.
Obviously, it's not my
real ladder.

There's a disease that's
been found in soft butter.
Doctors say it spreads
very easily.

Dijon vu - the same mustard as before.

I know lemons are sharp but try using one to carve a turkey.

I'd have a coffee, but it's not my cup of tea.

Venison's dear, isn't it?

My wife cooked me a full breakfast yesterday but forgot the toast. I couldn't help it; I went berserk. It turns out I'm lack toast intolerant.

Male cribs. They should be boycotted.

TV is called a medium because anything well done is rare.

The soap Casualty is now in its twenty-sixth year. Ironically, it's not getting any better.

So I bought this DVD, and in the Extras it said 'Deleted Scenes. When I had a look, there was nothing there.

'Doctor, I've hurt my arm in several places.' 'Well, don't go there anymore.'

My horse doesn't go out much. He's a shire horse.

What's got twelve legs, one eye, and four tails? Three blind mice and half a kipper.

People who get abducted by extraterrestrials can't really tell anyone.

They must feel so alienated.

Serial killer jokes aren't funny unless you execute them well.

To tell the difference between a chemist and a plumber, you ask them to pronounce "unionized."

George's model airplane hobby really took off.

The overreacting Watermelon was being melondramatic.

The royal family moved into my neighborhood. They live Tudors down.

Why are telescopes pointed away from Earth? Because they search for intelligent life

Did you see the horse that could balance a corncob on its head? It was some unique corn.

A horse walks into the counselor's office Mussels.

Why do bears have
hairy coats?

Fur protection.

What do you get when
you merge Iron Man
with a tire?

A Ferrous wheel

What runs faster, cold
or hot? Hot, because
you can catch a cold!

When Magnesium and Oxygen started dating, I was like, "OMG!"

How Do Hens Encourage Their Baseball Teams?

They egg them on!

I'm a lawyer, and my wife and I got in a fight recently because she was fed up with my very particular brand of humor.

What did Darth Vader say when his car broke down three miles outside of town? The empire hikes back

What do you call the Spanish translation of the 9th star wars movie? Rogue Juan.

I got caught sneaking onto a train once. I told the security guard that the price wasn't fare.

What does a car have when it's very itchy?

A road rash

Why was the squirrel late for work?

The traffic was nuts.

What happens when a plaster delivery truck wrecks and spills a load during rush hour? You get stucco in traffic.

What did the car say after it crashed? Ouch, that was wheely unfortunate.

Who's the Best Traffic Signal Superhero?

Green Arrow

When I fly, I like to hang air fresheners in the plane. It helps with descent.

What sound does a 747 makes when it bounces?

Boeing, Boeing.

Biggest cause of road rage?

Crossroads.

Traffic lights on my road have broken. No change there.

I never thought my brother would try to steal my job as a road worker. Then I started seeing the signs.

"The jokes were funny at first," she said. "But they're getting old! All you do is make courthouse puns!" "Guilty," I said.

I watched hockey before. It was cool. It was swimming. I watched swimming.

Enter a new password: 'chicken' I've got my ion you.

Why did Microsoft PowerPoint cross the road? To get to the other slide.

Batman walks into a superhero-only pool, and he is quickly stopped by a guard; the guard points to a sign that says, "No swimming without supervision."

What's a cow's favorite color?

Blooooo!

What kind of self-help books do dolphins read? Leading a porpoise-driven life

My brother is trying to fit the most elephants, geese, and bulls ever in a vintage music shop... He's breaking all sorts of records.

What does a zombie vegetarian eat?

GRRRAAAIINS!

I have this bad habit of kicking ice cubes under the refrigerator when they fall on the floor.

When is a door, not a door?

When it's ajar.

Sometimes, my friends don't believe I'm Jewish. When I tell them, they say, "No way! And I just respond, "Yahweh."

Those who jump off into the Paris river are in Seine.

I got arrested at the Farmers Market for disturbing the peas.

My son didn't tell me he ate some glue. His lips were sealed.

Did you hear about the school that converted to Marxism? I heard they don't have any classes.

Giant squid jokes are Kraken me up!

Looks like I lost an electron; I should keep a better ion them.

Don't trust atoms. They make up everything!

Opera enthusiasts are the Fandom of the Opera.

I got robbed on an elevator. That was wrong on so many levels!

DAD: I have found fault with an English word, and I need an entomologist! MOM: Don't you mean an etymologist? DAD: No, it's a bug, not a feature.

What's the favorite computer place for astronauts to hang out? At the space bar.

'Dad, are we pyromaniacs?'

'We arson.'

30% of car accidents in Sweden involve a moose. I say don't let them drive.

Two dead canaries on eBay.

They're not going cheep.

I do portraits of boxers. I can knock them out really quickly.

I saw this extinct bird with a hunchback. It was Quasidodo.

'Doctor, I keep thinking people are ignoring me.' 'Next!'

'Doctor, I keep getting the urge to purchase a big white bear from the Arctic.' 'You've got buy polar disorder.'

I just watched a documentary on the uses of the pick axe. It was ground breaking stuff.

'Doctor, I keep dreaming. My eyes change color.' 'It's just a pigment of your imagination.'

'Doctor, could you give me something for my liver?' 'Would half a pound of onions be OK?'

Last night I slept like a baby. I woke up three times, wet myself twice, and cried myself back to sleep.

As a family, we couldn't decide whether to have our granny cremated or buried, so in the end, we let her live.

So I said to this bloke, 'My favorite color's a bluey green.' He said, 'Azure.' I said, 'I'm certain.'

Interesting fact of the day. A steak and kidney pie in Barbados will cost you £2.50, and a mince and onion pie in St Lucia will cost you £3.00.

This spaceship landed in front of me, and out of it stepped a 5 metre diameter cream bun. It was one of those extra cholesterols.

Most pizza jokes are pretty cheesy.

I remember once we had a candlelit dinner. Everything was undercooked.

I've got an eating disorder. I go coffee first, then pudding, and then the main course.

What is the world's most favorite wine? 'I don't like Brussels sprouts'.

I spent most of today pruning. I was just chucking prunes at people.

I'm a three-times-a-night man. That toilet light is hardly ever off.

I know a man who's got jelly in one ear and custard in the other. He's a trifle deaf.

I've just started up an STD clinic from scratch.

What goes around, comes around. Look at Swingball.

What's most dangerous about swimming pools? Depends......

I've just been on a once-in-a-lifetime holiday. Never again!

I went on a holiday with my horse. It was self-cantering.

I'm no lifeguard but your baewatch me.

How do you define a farmer? Someone who's good in their field.

What type of medicine do ants use when they have eye problems? Ant-eye-biotics.

What type of haircut
do bees get?

Buzzcuts!

Why is the Mississippi
River unusual? Because
it has four eyes and
can't see!

Teacher: "John, where
are the Great Plains?"
John: "At the airport."

Don't trust that big cat.
He's lion.

Why did the crab
never share? Because
he's shellfish.

Why did the burglar
hang his mug shot on
the wall? To prove that
he was framed!

When do doctors get angry? When they run out of patients.

Every day I tell my wife I'm going to jog around the neighborhood, but I never do. It's a running joke, I have.

Somebody stole all my lamps. I couldn't be more de-lighted!

A boiled egg is hard to beat.

The shoe said to the hat, "You go on ahead, and I'll follow on foot."

What goes through every village, over mountains, crosses rivers and deserts, and yet never moves? A road.

Ever heard the rope joke? Skip it.

If a rabbit raced a cabbage, which would win? The cabbage because it's a head.

When I started telling dad jokes like my father, I knew I was full-groan.

A lorry carrying onions has overturned on the M62. Police are urging motorists to find a hard shoulder to cry on.

Lance Armstrong has denied ever using drugs, but he admitted pedaling.

It has recently been discovered that Wales is sinking into the sea due mainly to all the leeks in the ground.

I bought some Bermuda shorts, and when I took them off, my underpants had disappeared.

30 million acres of rainforest are being destroyed every year, and here I am attempting to recycle a single jar of Marmite.

The supermarket checkout sign said, 'Eight items or less.' So I changed my name to Les.

Everyone has the right to be stupid. Politicians just abuse the privilege.

Can deaf people tell the difference between a yawn and a scream?

I painted a picture of my cat's feet today. You could say it was a paw-trait.

An escalator can never break. It can only become stairs.

I've tried telling a few jokes about the unemployed, but they don't work.

Whatever you're do, always give 100%. Unless you're giving blood.

I couldn't find my favorite tv show.

I guess it was Lost.

How do you tune a fish?

With its scales!

What is a physicist's favorite food?

Fission chip.

Who's a cow's favorite person?

Youuuuuu!

Kid: "Ow! That hurt!" Dad: "What's wrong?" Kid: "I stubbed my toe!" Dad: "Oh no! Do you want me to call the toe truck?"

There was an inspirational song playing in the car that kept telling me to go the extra mile. Now I'm out of gas, and I don't know where I am.

I just got fired from the flower shop. Apparently, I took too many leaves.

How to get straight A's?

By using a ruler!

Why was the baby in Egypt?

It was looking for its mummy.

I was a bookkeeper for 10 years. The local librarians weren't too happy about it.

What is an astronaut's favorite key on a computer keyboard?

The space bar.

I'm proper Anglo-Welsh. My parents burnt down their own cottage.

What anti-perspirant do pessimists use?

Not Sure

TV is called a medium because anything well done is rare.

The soap Casualty is now in its twenty-sixth year. Ironically, it's not getting any better.

People who get abducted by extraterrestrials can't really tell anyone.

They must feel so alienated.

Serial killer jokes aren't funny unless you execute them well.

I can't believe that the penguin was denied bail. He's not even a flight risk!

I live in an airport, but when the security guard comes at night, Heathrows me out.

The best jokes about oranges have a tang of truth in them.

Why do bears have hairy coats?

Fur protection.

When Magnesium and Oxygen started dating, I was like, "OMG!"

Apparently, I snore too loud. It scared everyone in the car I was driving.

Biggest cause of road rage?

Crossroads.

Made in United States
Troutdale, OR
12/03/2023

15283776R00056